LIVING FRUGA

Tips on Saving Money and Living within Your Means

By Pepper Rosanne

Table of Contents

Living Frugally!

Living frugally is a state of mind; it is a way of seeing the choices you make and understanding how to fix them for the lowest and best price possible! I priced this book for under $5, so that like the techniques and philosophy my book advocates, its price isn't a burden on you. Since the whole point of this book is to RELIEVE that crushing burden of debt, not add to it!

Here you will learn powerful, not very well known and often times overlooked, common sense techniques to curve your spending and INCREASE your savings! This is the name of the game; from how to change the way you think about money, techniques on haggling, overlooked resources for savings, how to make a coupon go a loooong way, and much more. I truly hope that in these difficult economic times this book may be that little thing that helps you out.

Thank you for your purchase! Let the savings begin!

Frugality Begins With your Mindset

You don't have to begrudge saving money. It also doesn't need to seem like work. In fact, many would be glad to tell you that it is actually fun! It is true that saving money and living frugally brings all sorts of unpleasant images to people. It might make you feel cheap, or like you've been deprived of life's pleasures. But if you meet people who live frugally, a lot have energetic ideas to frugal living that makes it fun, and almost like a sport. No matter the amount of money saved, it's a penny to be used in the future, and can become a point of pride for many people. I began this wonderful journey by seeing if I could lower my electric bill. And with very little effort, I did it. And I was proud. Then came the heating costs. I saved money again. Then driving costs. Bam! Another victory.

Frugal living doesn't have to be painful on a family if you agree to take the attitude of having to do it. Like cleaning up the living room or bathroom. At first it's a pain, but it has to be done. Eventually you become accustomed to it, then maybe, it can be enjoyable. Maybe cleaning even becomes the moment of the day that you're able to meditate and relax. This is the attitude that will help you most when living frugally and make it as painless as possible. Living frugally and saving money doesn't just help your expenses, but many financial counselors and advisors agree that when people gain control of their money, they also gain control of their lives. The reason being that a strong sense of self-control moves over into other facets of your life, making you look at life differently. There are many reasons why you may have bought this book, and they are all legitimate, but the simplest thing you can start with is to pick one area you want to save money in, and focus on that. Then move to another needed area, and so on. As time progresses, you will find that that the very way you look at things will change. And as you get more experienced, and your vision changes, you'll begin to see new and fun ways to save money. And the best part of it all? It'll be effortless.

Spring Cleaning your Expenses!

There are so many small and large ways to save money, no matter the amount that you earn or have, that the results will blow you away! All you need to know is were to pinpoint the areas that can use some trimming. First thing; eliminate ALL of your unnecessary expenses. Things like eating out on weekends, buying lunch at work every day, subscribing to a bunch of magazines and newspapers that you barely read anyway, or even cutting down on your cable plan to eliminate the extra cost that unwatched channels rack up. These little steps might seem drastic at first, but once you really start noticing what you use and what you don't, the savings will magically appear. It's ok to reward and treat yourself and your family once in a while, but if you are serious about saving money, every penny counts!

Some other ways to reduce expenses would include looking at your checkbook and credit cards statements for any purchases that seem frivolous or unnecessary. Calling your credit card companies to see if they can lower you interest rates is also a good idea. This will help you to start looking more carefully at where you're hard earned dollars go every month, making it so your savings continue to grow month by month as you cut more and more waste.

Now, for those expenses that are necessary and you can't eliminate, it time to shop around for the best deals and maximize the amount of purchase-per-dollar. Looking up the best deals can seem like a pain, but when it comes to car insurance, groceries, and clothing, they can all be found at very low prices that will save you hundreds of dollars a month. All it takes is the time to look for them. The same can be applied to other monthly expense areas, such as: telephone and internet services, other types of insurance, mortgages, and even utility bills.

Saving money first comes from taking a hard look at what priorities take precedent in your life, and what savings goal you'd like to achieve. Taking the above steps will get you on a path to saving hundreds a month, and possibly even thousands every year. Just take the time and you'll see the results. It'll be well worth it in the long run.

Never Underestimate the Power of the Coupon!

As the retailers face more competition to keep costumers buying at their stores, especially in these tight times, they encourage customers to remain loyal by giving out coupons. These coupons can be extremely helpful when it comes to saving money, and I'm sure we have all used one before if we shop at big retailers. The magic of using coupons comes into play when you can identify stores that double or triple the face value of a coupon by finding ALREADY discounted items that are coupon compatible. Some stores only offer double or triple coupon values on specific days, so make sure to find out when they are and log them on your calendar. The amount of money this method can slash out of your grocery bill will amaze you.

But with great coupons, comes great vigilance. It extremely important you make sure the store isn't inflating the prices on their items and that you don't use coupons on these, since the rate of savings won't be very much. Along with that, don't be tempted to use a treasure trove of coupons on items you don't normally use, it might be tempting, but doing this might actually make your grocery bill go up higher!

You can find coupons in magazines, newspaper ads, or in the mail. But actually going to the website of the products or the store that you normally purchase items from may bring fruitful savings, with coupons that can be mailed to you or printed at home. If you have a smart phone, some sites will actually send you coupons on your phone! So if these sites offer opt-in lists for future promotions and coupons by email, you should set up a separate email account specifically for your opt-in's and take advantage of the deals. Also, make sure to keep track of when coupons expire, you may find that different coupons overlap each other's dates, and at these intersections the amount of savings can be incredible, but read the fine print to make sure you can do this.

Staying organized is highly important when it comes to serious coupon collecting. Creating a filing system with categories that are most applicable to you would be ideal. Using mini-filing binders or buying those clear plastic pages with holes for three ring binders would great. Colored post it notes will help you get organize too. Get creative and use whatever feels more natural to you. But make sure that its travel accessible, since you will be finding yourself taking your folder with you to the grocery store quite a few times.

Many retailers are so willing to keep you as a customer, that if you take a competitors coupon into a store and ask the manager to match, or even do better than the competitor's price, they will. The best way to go about doing this is to ask for the manager and explain that you really want to make a purchase from them, but the competitors store offers a better deal. This will usually get them to match the price, or even beat it, just to have you stay a loyal customer. Never underestimate the power the customer can have.

Now, besides grocery stores, there are many coupons that can be found for other things as well. Whenever you plan to visit an amusement park, museum, or other activity, check first to see if coupons are available. More often than not there are buy-one-get-one-free deals when it comes to events, shows, and the like. Looking online for these deals would be the best route, or you can call your chamber of commerce in the area of the event to see if they have any options. Even buying discounted tickets on online auctions like ebay or yahoo will give you a large and diverse inventory of savings. Just make sure the tickets and vendor are legitimate and trusted (by their ratings, or stars, on ebay) and that they get them to you on time!

Restaurants like to offer lots of discounts to get people in to eat, and taking advantage of these opportunities can offer you and your family a nice little outing for a fair price. But make sure to pay a close eye to the details of the coupon. Many restaurants will only allow the coupons on specific days or even specific hours on a specific day! So jot the times and days down and plan accordingly.

Taking the time to find coupons for things that you already buy will reap you massive savings. Sure, maybe using a $.75 cent or $ 2.00 coupon here and there may seem trivial, but when it becomes a habit, and by the end of the year those thousand dollar grocery bills no longer look as large as they used to, you'll realize just how much little savings really add up!

Discount Stores? Really?

Dollar stores and other discount stores are increasingly popping up. Most likely the town you live in has one nearby. The reason for their popularity is obvious, and if you really want to save money, using these stores for certain items can really give your wallet a break. If you think these stores sell cheap quality goods, you'd be right. But they also have good quality items. And in all honesty, the level of quality is trivial considering what you might need to buy anyway. I mean, if you can't do without your $7 pack of premium comfort kleenex, then most likely this book's not for you.

So, with that said, what kinds of things can you buy at dollar and discount stores? Well, for starters how about special event cards? A lot of these can cost as much as $3 or more at most retailers, but at dollar and discount stores you can get them for $.50 or cheaper. They are still funny, sentimental, and cute. They won't show their discounted price if you gave them to anyone.

Disposable items for parties are also vastly cheaper at dollar stores. When you buy napkins, cups, silverware, paper plates, invitation, tablecloths, even chips, condiments and food at brand retailers, we could be talking about a possible triple figure amount! Dollar stores sell all this for pennies on the dollar and the products still get the job done just as effectively. Wrapping paper and gift bags are also very cheap at discount stores.

When you're getting gifts for family or friends I wouldn't recommend going to discount stores as your first choice. Unless your friends and family are ok with cheaper presents, it's your prerogative. Myself, I like to buy picture frames from dollar stores. They look nice and are incredible cheap, I once bought a set of three that looked like glass, but if someone really cared to inspect them they would see they were plastic. They look great on my dresser though! This is how it plays out with things bought at discount stores, they are good items and look nice, but if you are preoccupied with brands and "authentic" products, you may have to pay an arm and a leg. But if you don't mind cheaper materials, using discount stores gives you great, nice looking things for practically free to decorate your home.

This also applies to toys. The toys at discount stores may break easily, but will provide good fun for your kids for a while. Now, a lot of kids want that cool new toy, but one thing that you can do to entice them to want one of the discount stores toys would be to tell them:

"Ok, I'll take you to buy that toy, but first let's see if there is anything you'll want at the dollar store instead, if not, I'll buy the toy, but if you get something, then that's all for today."

Something along the lines of this dialogue will almost always get your kids to want something in the dollar store compared to the "cool new thing". Because after all, kids want instant gratification, and between a brightly colored nerf sword or doll that is right in front of them at the dollar store, and toy far off in the future, they'll go for the dollar toy every time! Also, because the toys are so much cheaper at dollar stores, you can get your kids a bunch of toys at a time. This will most always convince your children to get the pile of toys instead of that "one" toy at the brand retailer. Great toys at dollar stores include bubbles, coloring books, marbles, sidewalk chalk, cards, gag toys and more.

Office supplies are also terribly over priced at brand retailers, and when it comes to school year, forget about it! Notbooks, paper, glue, pens, scissors, rulers, calculators, envelopes, binders and more are all available at discount stores for half if not 75% cheaper! Plus, the quality of these items even rivals that of normal stores.

So when it comes to bargains, never underestimate the saving power of dollar and discount stores.

The Flea Market Treasure Hunt!

I love spending hours and hours on a nice Sunday morning browsing the interesting and unique treasures of the local flea market. There are lots of new and used items at flea markets, and the great thing about it is that you can haggle for a great price! You never really know what great things you can find at a flea market, but that's what makes it fun. Some of the things you can expect to find? Homemade crafts, clothing, shoes, jewelry, toys, video games, tools, furniture, antiques, bikes, and much, much more.

To make your flea market trip the best it can be, bring a hat and sunscreen, since most are outdoors. There are some indoors, it just depends were you are. Its good to bring a large bag, canvas one or something like it, that can hold some weight is good. You can also purchase cheap carts to make transporting goods easier.

Good walking shoes are a must, so you don't have to end your day early. A good hunting tip is to start at the back of the flea market and work your way up to the entrance, so that you end up with you load near your vehicle and shorten the walk. An added bonus too is that you will be able to have the pick of the good things in the back, since everyone tends to start at the front.

Going to the flea market early in the morning is best time to get the best items, since the real traffic hasn't come through yet. The only bad thing about this is that it's harder to haggle down the prices. By the end of the day vendor will be much more malleable since they don't want to pack up more things than they have too. If you have a specific item in mind, and you can wait until later in the day, you'll get a better price. But the risk of it being bought fist is also there. Personally I prefer to go early in the morning and haggle. There is never any harm in asking for a lower price and you might get it, so be fearless in this regard. Asking the vendor what the lowest price is for an item will usually get you a good deal, but if you do want to make a lower offer, make sure to have the money in your hand out for them to see. This entices the vendor to want to sell.

If you really want to get methodical about it, you can even bring a pad and pen and write down the table numbers of items you want, but are too expensive. Then at the end of the day, you return to those tables and check if you can get a cheaper price.

Early Bird gets the Worm! Garage Sale Deals!

How does that saying go? Ones man's trash is another man's treasure? Well, when it comes to garage sales, this motto can't be anymore more true. Though the "trash" you can find at garage sales are actually more along the spectrum of high-end, collectable, modern, even brand new brand name quality items. This is one of the greatest places to find great items that you can not only use in your home, but can actually sell for a profit on sites like Ebay.

The great thing about garage sales is the bargain. You can almost always get a rock bottom prices by asking for it, or talking them into it. But don't insult them with a ridiculous price when something is obviously of greater value. Most of the times though, the great things that you find at garage sales that may sell for $20 or $40 in stores, you can get for 10 bucks or less! If you really want something, but the seller won't budge, you can always give them you number and ask them to call you later if the item doesn't sell. Most people just want to get rid of their stuff as fast as possible so they don't have to repack it, store it, or donate it. Bundling items and offering a group price is also a good strategy.

Finding the best items is key in making your Saturday worthwhile. Starting early in the morning is best, since you will be able to get first pick. Printing out all the ads and creating a route will help you maximize the number of sales you will visit without wasting time gas and backtracking. It can be fun traveling with a friend or family member, or even by yourself, since each garage sale is like a new treasure trove just waiting to be picked!

The items you can find at garage sales vary but common things you can find are furniture, baby products, kitchen products, art, tools, clothing (sometimes *really* expensive, brand names outfits for virtually nothing), shoes, purses, makeup (sometimes unopened) sports equipment, toys, bikes, video games, electronics, tv's, game consoles, even vehicles sometimes.

Really, there is an endless amount of things you can find. Chances are if you need or want something, you will be able to buy it at a garage sale eventually.

Career clothes are extremely expensive but you can find a great selection of high quality work clothes, both men and women, at garage sales. I've even come across business suites that still had their tags on them. I couldn't try on all the clothes of course, but when I can pick up a $60 skirt and top set for $2.50, I'll take a chance, thank you very much!

When looking for furniture, zone in on ads that describe estate or moving sales. Most of the time they will try to sell everything so they won't have to pack up. Generally, you can even get them to help you load the items too. If you are local, sometimes they will even deliver. Otherwise, make sure to have a big enough vehicle. You can also ask to come back later, when you have made arrangements with whoever you can ask for help, and pick it up. The seller will be happy to hold a paid item for a few hours.

Enjoy your time going to garage sales! It's a great way to find great things; get rock bottom prices and meet new and interesting people!

I don't know...aren't Pawn Shops...Scary?

Haha, no. Despite what some seedy movies might want you to believe, pawn shops are not scary at all, and actually have incredible deals!

Sometimes you might really want that one luxurious item that just wasn't in your budget. If these feelings do come up, then pawn shops are a great solution. Local pawn shops typically have lots of high value items for a fraction of their original cost.

Also, pawn shops are a great way to get quick cash or loans if you need them. To get cash is simple; you bring in something, and if the pawn shop owner wants it, you sell it. This is great way to get rid of extra jewelry, old watches and other extra things you don't use anymore. If you want to get a loan, all you need to do is bring something in, ask for a lump sum of cash for it, and if the pawn shop owner agrees, he will loan you the money with the understanding that if you don't come back in a month to repay the loan (with some interest) he will have the legal right to sell it. The interest amount varies by state and local regulations and you can ask the pawn shop owner about all terms and conditions. This is a great method for getting quick cash to pay off immediate credit card, other debts, or just have needed spending money, but still have a chance to get back that favorite thing you pawned back.

Items in pawn shops are in a constant state of flux, so visit often to see what new merchandise they might have received.

The most common things found at pawn shops may include guns, vcr's, tv's, dvd players, dvds, video games/consoles, cameras, tools, jewelry, furniture, watches, music, and musical instruments. But those are only the common things, sometimes rarer items can be found like; celebrity autographs, historical antiques, collectables and more. If you're looking for a very specific item and they don't have it, you can give them you phone number and ask them to call you if it comes in. Most pawn shop owners will be kind enough to oblige.

The majority of the things in pawn shops are in very good condition. The reason being that most of the people who take their items to pawn shops would still be using the items, if not for their need of money. Many people do come back to pick up their items, but some either can't pay, or never had the intention of picking the item up. The things you find in pawn shops can be of amazing quality, while still saving you a buck!

Pawn shop owners are under legal obligation to get the information of whomever purchases and sells and item. This is done in case something that is sold is stolen, or if the police need to track down someone who bought something. For the most part you won't have any problems buying things at pawn shops. I never have.

When it comes to buying a gun at a pawn shop, you'll have to get ready to do all the paper work that it would take to buy a new gun. Most states have mandatory waiting periods before you can take the gun, and pawn shops have to follow the same rules.

Pawn shops are a great resource to find high quality things for good prices. But make sure to carefully inspect everything before purchase as they usually don't have a warranty.

Great Deals at Antique Shops?! Get Outta Here!

Many have the idea that antiques and antique shops cost more than they can afford. But this is not so. Browsing a good antique store is a great way to spend a lazy afternoon and I guarantee you that you will be amazed at the great deals to stumble across!

One of the hardest things about antique shopping is that we may not know the true value of some items. The item may have caught your fancy because of its design, or maybe it brought back nostalgic memories, but knowing whether the shop owner is upping the price is tricky. The only way to overcome this uncertainty is to come to a maximum price you'd be willing to pay, and if the shop owner won't sell it, walk away. It may be hard, but having a will of steel is a must if you want to get serious about saving money.

Doing some information gathering on the antique dealer before you even go into their store is also good idea. Getting to know the store owner might get you some good deals you wouldn't have been able to get otherwise. If you are a frequent shopper in the store this will also help you build a relationship, and if you really want to get on the good side of the owner, bringing in new customers will definitely get you noticed. This can lead to the owner giving you good deals so that you keep generating business for them, especially in this economy.

Typically you will be able to negotiate for the prices of things you want, but usually only if the antique store is run by the owner or the owners family members. Going to antique malls may have a larger selection, but it won't get you much leeway in haggling since they may be run by hired employees with no ties to the owner. I prefer, family owned and run, antique stores since they offer better prices and they can even provide you a bit of history on items you purchase!

Money talks. So carry a good amount of cash when looking for antiques. It will take the hassle out of credit a card transaction (which they may not even support) or personal checks (which older antique stores won't even take).

It's important to check the condition that the antiques are in before you purchase. Thoroughly inspecting them will take the surprises out of buying from antique stores. The last thing you want is to buy something, take it home, then realize it's missing something or that it's on the verge of breaking, thinking you got a good deal. Most reputable antique dealers will take pride in having only high quality items, but always check just to make sure.

Looking online for certain antiques, noting its online prices, and then negotiating for about 25% less at antique stores is a good method to get good deals. Be fearless in this regard. It also helps to say things along the lines of "Would you take $100 for this?" and show them the money, instead of "Can you lower the price?" The first example is more direct and forceful, and showing them the money entices them to take the deal. The second method is passive and leaves the control with the seller and not you, the buyer.

Saving Money at the Pump!

With the cost of gas going up, and the unstable Middle East, finding ways to save gas is a big deal! Here I'm going to list some small, big, and even some EXTREME solutions to save you money at the pump:

Get a gas card: Most, if not all major gas stations offer some kind of gas credit card which will let you save 3-5% on every gas purchase you make at their stations. If it takes $45 to fill up a tank of gas, then at 5% you will save $2,25. It might not seem like a lot, but if you have to fill up every week, and you multiply that by 54 weeks, you can save $121.50! Not bad, don't you think?

Don't be an aggressive driver: Hitting the gas pedal like a racecar driver when the light turns green or braking hard will increase your gas consumption and frequency of fill ups.

Cruise control: Cruise control help you drive at a steady speed with no speed fluctuations that use up gas. You could see an average 7% savings in gas usage by using this method.

Hold your horses: Going fast gets your adrenaline pumping and makes you feel like a daredevil, but it also can rack you up a nice pile of tickets and gas receipts. So slow down and conserve.

"Idle hands" and all that: If you're sitting and waiting in your car, either for someone to get out of a store or for whatever reason, save yourself some money and turn the engine off. It also goes without saying that if you can avoid rush hour traffic, do it.

Plan ahead: Mapping out the places and route you need to go for the shortest possible traveling time will save you time and money.

We all have legs, time to put them to use: If you can walk somewhere instead of driving, or even riding a bike, try doing it.

Get an electric car: This is a bigger solution, but with electric cars coming out, such as the Chevy volt, Nissan leaf, and cars from Tesla Motors, it will wipe out your gas consumption completely. These cars get great mileage that is more than enough for 90% percent of daily driving tasks around your home town (which uses up gas the most) and only cost about $2-4 to completely charge the car. If you were comparing this price to gasoline prices, if would cost you 75 cents a gallon! Now that's saving! You can also get tax breaks if you buy a hybrid or electric car. Take a look at them and you will be pleasantly surprised at their affordable prices.

Public transportation: Many times you can get monthly passes that are affordable and are well worth the cost compared to how much gas you would have to pay for.

Extreme ways to save gas:

- Filling up your car at 3 in the morning or earlier when it is very cool will save you money. Why? The reason is that gas gets denser when it cools, and pumps charge you by volume, not density. So you get a bit more for your buck.

- Drive with the a/c off and windows rolled up. This improves the car's aerodynamics and lowers drag and how hard you car has to work to move.

- Replace your air filter, keep your tires aligned and inflated, and tune your engine. All these little tweaks will improve your gas mileage by around ten percent.

- Rolling through stop signs. This is DANGEROUS and ILLEGAL. I DO NOT ADVOCATE DOING THIS. It is up to you to use caution and common sense. But doing this will remove the gas consumption need to accelerate after breaking.

- Turning off your car while it's still moving: The American Automobile Association warns against using this technique, but bloggers and green enthusiasts do promote it. But remember: THIS CAN BE VERY DANGEROUS if you haven't practiced. Practice in wide open spaces with no cars or people around to get used to driving without power steering. The idea of this technique is to use the cars momentum to go downhill or glide into parking spaces without using gas. This is only to be used at SLOW SPEEDS, NEVER AT HIGH SPEEDS!

- Use alternative fuels in your car. This will have to be researched extensively, but some are using filtered cooking oil taken from fast food chains and using it as fuel.

Getting Good Deals from Uncle Sam!

You might not know it, but Uncle Sam gets a whole lot of stuff from its citizenry. When houses are sold at government auctions, or when stolen things are confiscated, or even when businesses go bankrupt, and for many other reasons, the government gets saddled with selling off all the goods. A lot of the times you can find things that come in "lots". What this means is that you might see a sale for 50 plasma screen tv's for a thousand bucks. You just need to bid and you can take it home! Each auction and its merchandise vary by state, but usually you can find cars, boats, electronics, and everything imaginable at these events!

Here are some helpful links to get you started:

http://www.publicsurplus.com/sms/browse/home

http://gsaauctions.gov/gsaauctions/gsaauctions/

http://www.govdeals.com/

http://www.govliquidation.com/

http://www.governmentauctions.org/FreeByStateAuctions.asp

Having Fun Being Frugal!

With all these savings that we have gone through, you might be asking yourself "Will I ever have any fun"?! The answer is a resounding yes! In this last section I'm going to give you some fun ideas on how to live it up frugally!

If you live in a good sized city, try taking a nice walk! You'd be surprised how many fun, impromptu concert or events you might find. I know I stumbled into some great street musicians! You can also hang out in the park with friends and watch people passing by. You'd be amazed how much fun it is!

Put a hold on eating out or going to bars with friends and instead have a potluck at home. It's cheaper to buy liquor than to buy drinks at a pricy bar.

When you want to go see movies, buy the matinee tickets or go see the $2 movies (some communities have this, check to see if yours is one of them). You can always rent movies too. College campuses, if you're near one, also have lots of free movie events and showings.

If you really want to cut back on expenditures, cable is a biggie. It can be really expensive. But, I can understand if you want it. In that case try to get the minimum number channels, or just get basic. Buying a nice DVD player and renting is cheaper than having cable in the long stretch. Though, if you're like me who rents rooms in your home, keep the cable, since it's a nice perk for the tenants.

Taking your kids to the library or bookstore and hanging out reading is a great way to have fun with no money spent. You can also get your kids involved in a community group. Things like theatre are great and help your children develop skill and make friends.

Look up event times for free community shows in the park and libraries. In the summer many events pop up. Write them down in a calendar.

Keep on Saving!

Thank you for reading this book! I hope that the ideas set forth have gotten you thinking about the many possible ways to cut down on your expenses and save money. The creative combinations and possibilities to saving money are endless, so get creative and don't give up!

Please take a minute to give my book an honest review, I would greatly appreciate it! I wish you the best in living frugally!

Made in the USA
Lexington, KY
20 May 2012